I can rhyme.
Can you?

Summer Ng.

Presentation by *BookLeaf Publishing*

Web: www.bookleafpub.com

E-mail: info@bookleafpub.com

ISBN: 978-93-95755-80-1

First edition 2022

Polar bear

Wild flowers on the field
Strongly and freely grow.
Look! There's a snowmobile
Coming so fast and close.

Oh! It doesn't have wheels,
But it has so big toes.
Is that a giant seal
Or a white buffalo?

Hang on - I think I know
It is a polar bear.
But it's not on the snow,
It's in the floral wear.

Sunshine

I love the spring sunshine
I soak in it sometimes.
But when it's time for night,
All the sunlight will hide.
I'll wait for the sunrise
The scene pleases my eyes.

I can rhyme. Can you?

Teacher: I can rhyme. Can you?
Student: I don't have a clue.
      Tell me what to do.
Teacher: Sure! Let us go through
      The important rule.

Teacher: "Clown" can rhyme with "town".
      They have the same sound.
      So you just write down
      Words with rhyming sounds.
      Wanna try it now?

Student: "Zoo" can rhyme with "blue".
      Now that I can do
      I'll make a breakthrough
      Become a guru.
      You can do it too.

The last leaf

Seeing the last leaf,
She has a belief.
When the last leaf falls,
Her life would be gone.

Much to her surprise,
After stormy nights,
The leaf still survives,
Which makes her alive.

...

There's a poor artist
Whose work's the greatest.
A leaf never falls,
A leaf on the wall.

(Based on the story "The last leaf" by O. Henry)

Fun rhymes

Rhyming is fun
It's like a bun
You will be stunned
By what you've done.

Little bee

I am a little bee
I look very carefree.
I really like flowers
I land on them for hours.
I'm not doing nothing
I'm really hard-working.
I'm a pollinator
Who collects the nectar.

Summer

On sunny days in the summer
I'm easy to be in anger.
It is time for me to pamper
Myself with a cool cucumber.

Motorbike

I have a motorbike
I ride it day and night.
It's always by my side.
It is my little guy
To whom I can confide
All secrets of my life.

Goose and Moose

There once was a goose
That liked drinking juice
And eating fresh fruits.
It was friends with moose.
They went on a cruise;
They put on new shoes.
Now they're in the news!

Sad

Today I am sad
I feel very bad.
So please don't get mad,
If I am not rad.

A slogging frog

Do you see the frog
Sitting on that log?
It prefers to slog
Around the peat bog
Where there is no smog.
If you like this frog,
Comment on my blog.

A break

Have a headache?
Let's take a break.
Sit by the lake
Eat a cupcake
Forget the stake
For your own sake.

Cat and Rat

13

My little cat
Had a fur hat.
It liked to chat
With a fat rat.

One day the rat
Entered combat
With my small cat
To take the hat.

Couldn't stand that,
I gave the hat
To a fruit bat.
"Stop the combat!"

Stampede

I want to see a stampede
The horses run at top speed.
They are the world's best horse breeds
That are fed on healthy weeds.
It's generally agreed
They're exceptional indeed.

Rhyming poem

When you have spare time,
Let's think of a rhyme.
Don't need to be strict
To make it perfect.
Just let your mind loose
So it can produce
Fun rhyming poems
With lovely rhythms.

Challenge

Now you know to rhyme
Do it anytime.
"Practice makes perfect",
To which you should stick.

Let's try this challenge
What rhymes with "orange"?
Accept the challenge
And don't start to whinge.

I'm sure it's easy
You'll solve it quickly.
"Syringe" and "lozenge"
Can rhyme with "orange".

Mommy is not home

Mommy is not home
She's going to Rome.
She will be back soon
Let's wait until noon.

...

She is still away
I don't want to play.
I wish she was back
And bought me a snack.

...

It is getting dark
I heard the dog bark
My mom has come home
And bought me a gnome.

Let's go fly a kite

Let's go fly a kite
And then grab a bite.
Enjoy the sunlight
When the sky is bright.

A simple delight
At a nice campsite
But it can excite
Happiness and might.

Fly

I want to fly
Into the sky
Fly up so high
Like a free guy.

Late

I used to be late
And let my friends wait.
I went to donate
Blood to my roommate.
Because I came late,
She had a long wait
And couldn't think straight.
So after that date,
I changed my bad trait.

Have fun

I wish I was an ......
Singing a lovely chant.
I wish I was a ......
Flying over the sea.
I wish I was a ......
Having a nice Kit Kat.
I wish I was a ......
Writing a travel blog.
I wish I was an ......
Getting behind the wheel.
I wish I was a ......
Eating a big hot-dog.
I wish I was a ......
Riding a sailing boat.
I wish I was a ......
Playing on a golf course.
I wish I was the ......
Freezing all ugly mice.
I wish I was a ......
Having a lunch buffet.
I wish I was a ......
Reaching a great height.
I wish I was a ......
Eating strawberry jam.
I wish I was a ......

Living in a dog house.
I wish I was a ......
Travelling with a snail.
I wish I was an ......
Being friends with wildfowl.
I wish I was a ......
Wearing a pretty wig.
I wish I was a ......
Visiting a blue whale.
I wish I was a ......
Wearing a giant hat.
I wish I was a ......
Eating yummy beefsteak.
I wish I was a ......
Jogging on a long road.
I wish I was an ......
Containing lots of fern.
I wish I was a ......
Digging big deep hole.
I wish I was a ......
Devouring some stale kale.
I wish I was "XO"
Hugs and kisses on snow.
I wish I was a yak
Eating a healthy snack.
I wish I had a zeal
To make this world ideal.

Suggested answers:
Ant, bee, cat, dog, eel, frog, goat, horse, ice, jay,
kite, lamb, mouse, nail, owl, pig, quail, rat,
snake, toad, urn, vole, whale